네 칸 그림에 당신의 마음을 담은

단 상 집

단상집

내 가 그대의 영혼에 마음을 담은

머리 속을 스치던 생각

가슴 속에 지녔던 감정

둘을 보시고 무엇을 채우시던 여러분의 자유입니다.

DREAM

UNDRESS

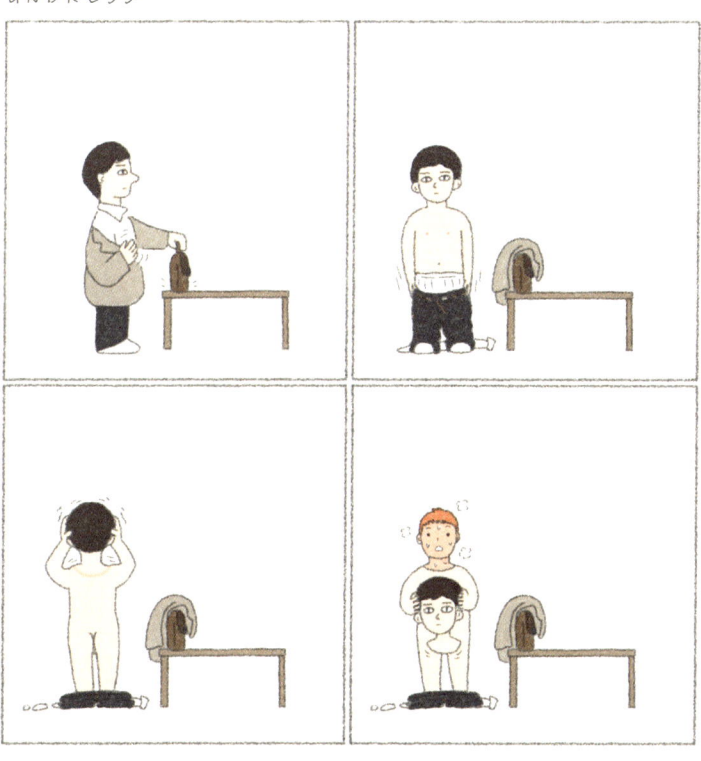

ORDER

HUNTING

DOG

POSITION

HOPE

STAR

COMPARE

WINNER

ASAP

WING

SMILE MAN

ADDICTION

UNFREE

NIGHT

ALIEN

FARMING

REFERENCE

TREND

BLAH

NOT LONELY

GAP

CLIMB

PRAYER

ARREST

JUST FRIEND

SECRET LOVE

BUD

PEACE

DESK

WARRIOR

CYCLE

FLY

PT

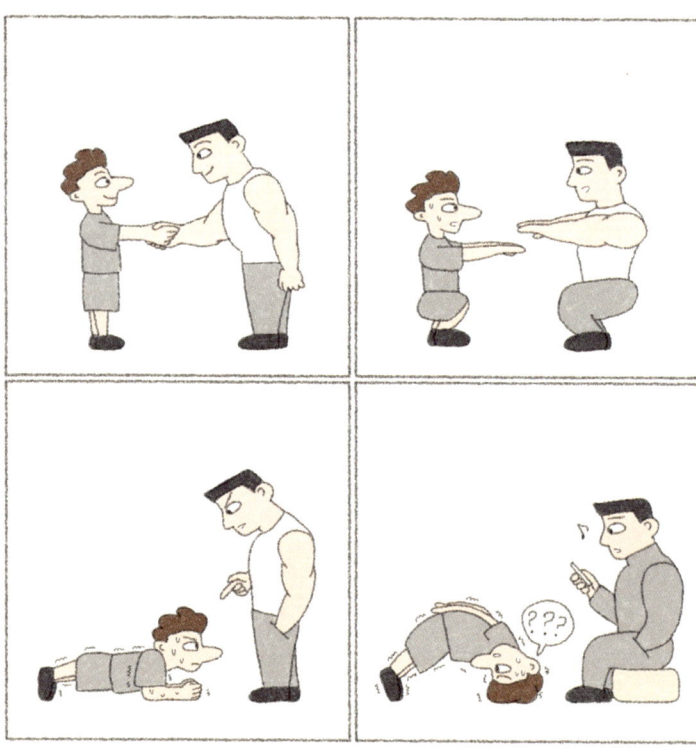

UNDERSTAND

LUCKY

SMOKE

KID

PART

MILK

FIRST

EAT

WEIGHT

DENTAL

TRUST

HOLIDAY

SLEEPING & RHYTHM

ERROR

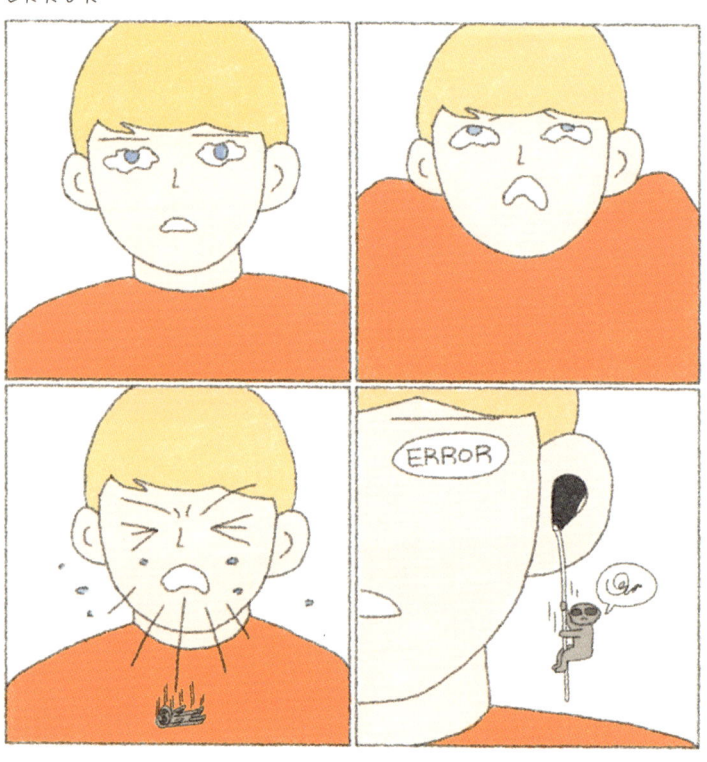

BIG ART

HOUSE

EGG

FEEDBACK

PEACH

SMART LOVE

BUTTERFLY EFFECT

PRAY ROBOT

HALLOWEEN

PERFUME

FORMAT

LOW BIRD

RABBIT'S STAR

ARROW

ANGEL(1)

ANGEL(2)

ANGEL(3)

PRECIOUS

MEET

HIDDEN

ANSWER

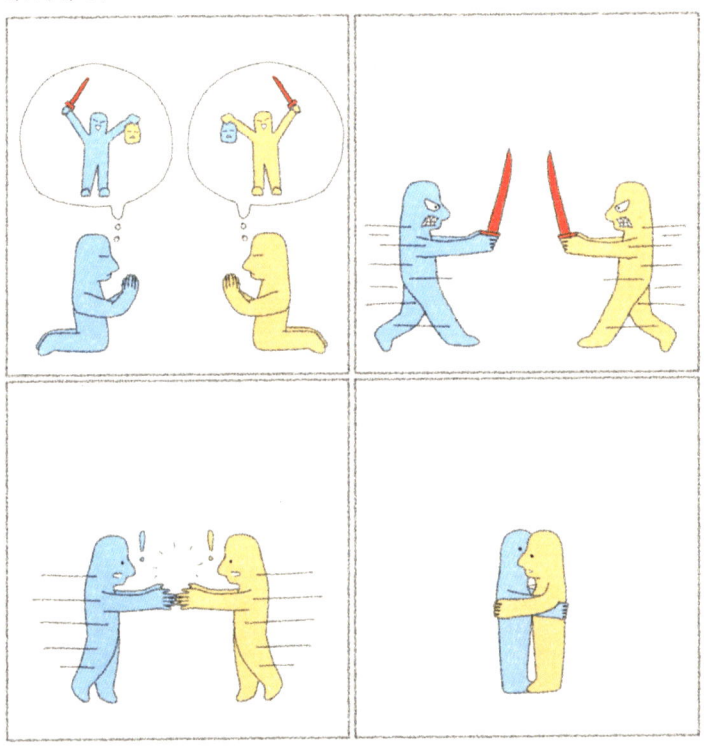

NEGO

WINTER CLOTHER

SNOWMAN

FIND

BOX

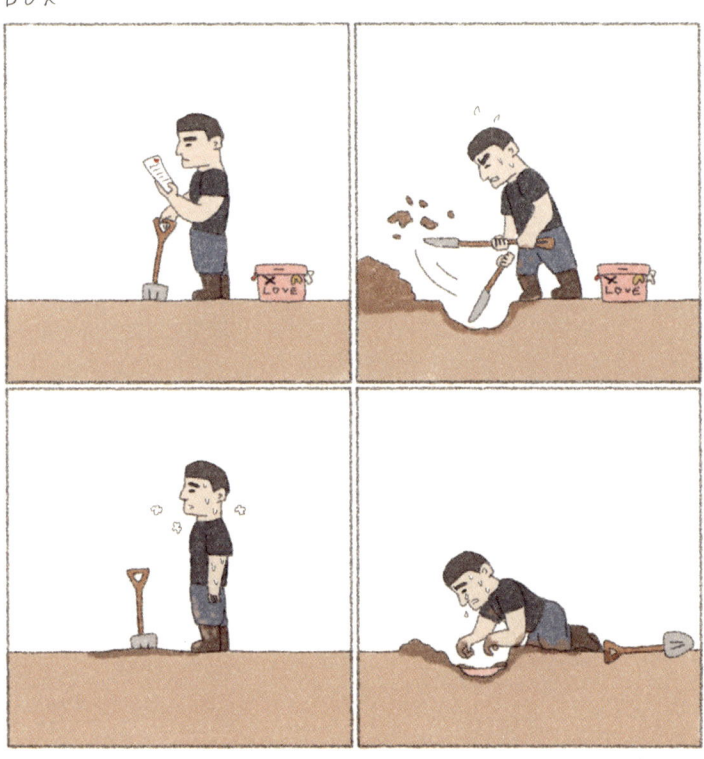

DRUNKEN

REMAINING MEMORY

1958

BIRTH

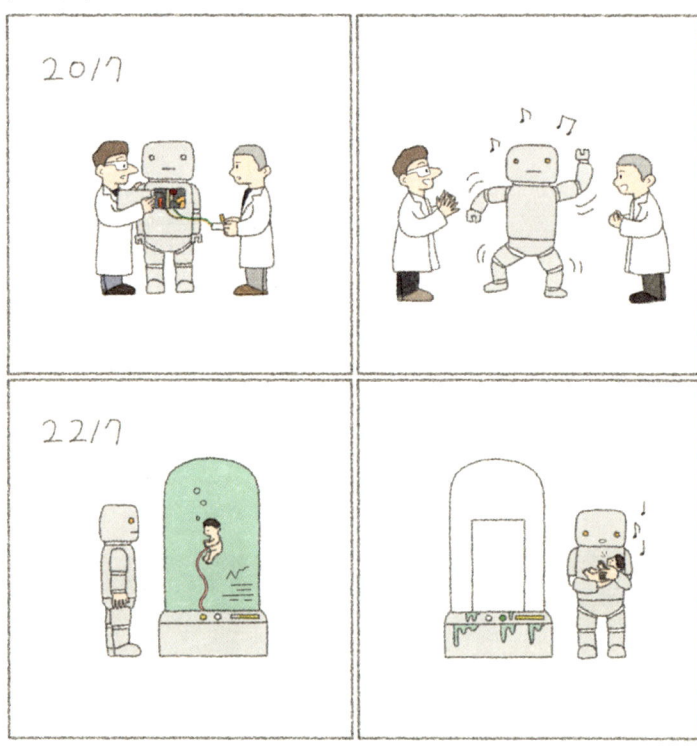

REBIRTH

DOING

MASTER

PANIC

TRAUMA

WEEKEND

MOUSE

DRILLER

SHOES

TRUCE

WITER MOSQUITO

LAZY

MOON

KIDDING

WINTER SLEEP

INDIVIDUALITY

DONATION

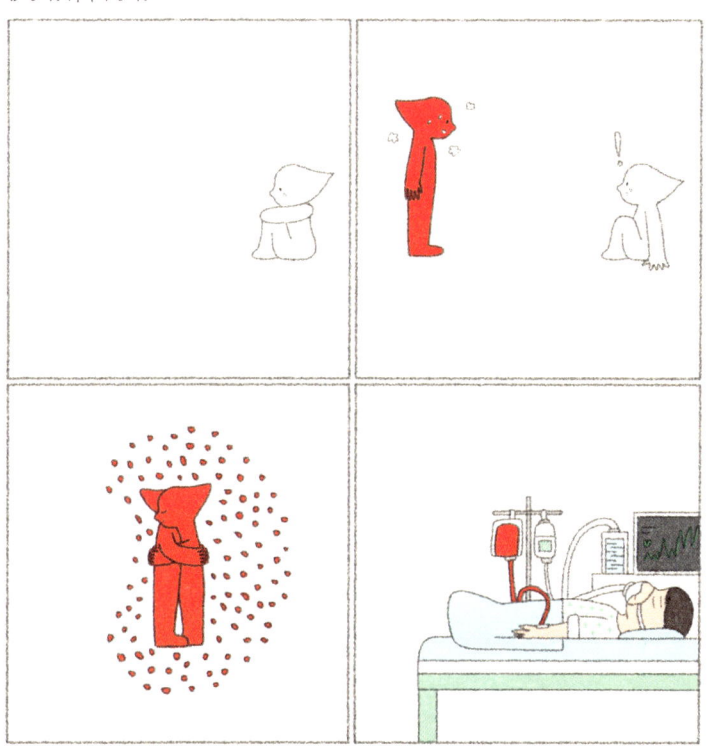

REMNANT

BLACK DOG

JAM

HIDDEN CHARACTER

ADVANCE

HEIGHT

GREEDY

NEW LIFE

ESCAPE

BAD HERO

MELT

GOLD DOG

STAKE

'지나온 날의 단상들'

포맷

가난

팀장

오디션

정도껏

처지

희망사항

당위성

파마

33

다이어트

안녕

바람

선택

불필요한 사랑

분노

절제

거짓말

민폐

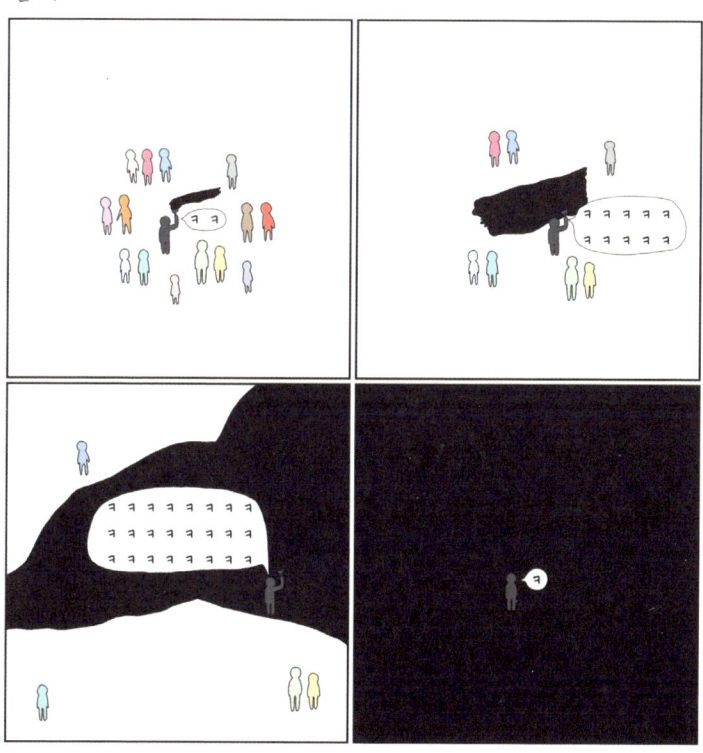

금요일

충격요법

어린이

목표

깊이

가치

자유

게으름

이루는 것

키

건너뛰기

좋아하는 일

미안하고 사랑해

밤

잠

이치

그의 갤러리

비밀

비

원하는 것

REMEMBER

달빛과 하늘과 꽃에게 이 책을 바칩니다.

네 칸 그림에 당신의 마음을 담은

단 상 집

글·그림　　최지환
펴낸이　　　박명천
펴낸곳　　　매스메스에이지

디자인　　　꽃피는 봄이오면
인쇄　　　　다보아이앤씨

주　소　　　강남구 논현로 139길 12 매스메스에이지
전화번호　　02 542 1848

ISBN　　　978-89-967180-4-8

2018년 02월 12일 초판 1쇄 2000부 인쇄
2018년 02월 19일 초판 1쇄 2000부 발행

Copyright ⓒ 2018 MASSMESSAGE

이 도서의 국립중앙도서관 출판예정도서목록(CIP)은 서지정보유통지원시스템 홈페이지
(http://seoji.nl.go.kr)와 국가자료공동목록시스템(http://www.nl.go.kr/kolisnet)에서
이용하실 수 있습니다. (CIP제어번호 : CIP2018003626)